Weddin

NOTEBOOK

Wedding Planner
NOTEBOOK

Planning Your Wedding Made Easy

Vera Tanger

iUniverse, Inc.
Bloomington

Wedding Planner Notebook
Planning Your Wedding Made Easy

iUniverse books may be ordered through booksellers or by contacting:

iUniverse
1663 Liberty Drive
Bloomington, IN 47403
www.iuniverse.com
1-800-Authors (1-800-288-4677)

ISBN: 978-1-4759-2631-6 (sc)
ISBN: 978-1-4759-2632-3 (ebk)

Printed in the United States of America

iUniverse rev. date: 06/06/2012

INTRODUCTION

Dear Bride,

You are engaged. Congratulations! After telling family and friends, the next step is to organize your wedding. It's an important task with 1,001 different things to do and remember.

The *Wedding Planner Notebook* works as a memory helper and a personal confidante where you will write down ideas, suppliers' contacts, and budget info, to list a few examples.

Live this period in harmony and joy without stress, and have everything ready on time.

Let's begin!

Location, date, and time of my wedding:

IDEAS
for my
WEDDING

Ideas for my Wedding

See something you like? Write it down for further reference, gather clippings, and make a note of good websites. When attending others' events, observe routines and put those you might use in writing. Every good idea counts.

MUSIC

MUSIC

Note song titles and composers to start compiling the different playlists needed for this special day. Also note each event and the music required: the ceremony, the reception, and the dance party—never forgetting your unique song and the first dance.

QUESTIONS

for

SUPPLIERS

QUESTIONS FOR SUPPLIERS

Looking for the right supplier and finding out about his or her professional competence is important and a guarantee for success. Bring up every question you may think necessary, confirm details, negotiate wisely, and write down the answers or get those answers in writing from the supplier.

BRIDAL BOUTIQUE

Name of boutique:

_____

Name and phone number of contact person:

_____

How many years have you been in business?

_____

What are your hours of operation?

_____

Are appointments needed?

_____

How long do appointments last?

_____

Is there a fee for trying on dresses?

_____

How many people can I bring along?

_____

How long will it take for the dress to be made?

_____

Do you offer any discounts or giveaways?

_____

What major bridal gown lines do you carry?

_____

What are their price ranges?

_____

Do you carry bridal shoes?

What are their price ranges?

Do you dye shoes to match outfits?

Do you carry outfits for the mother of the bride?

Do you carry bridesmaids' gowns?

Do you carry tuxedos and morning coats or men's suits?

Do you carry outfits for the flower girl and ring bearer?

Do you offer in-house alterations? If not, do you have any recommendations?

How many fittings will I need?

What do I need to bring for the fitting session?

Are coordinating accessories available?

What is the estimated date of delivery for my gown?

What exactly is included?

Are there any additional fees?

_____

How much is the deposit?

_____

What is the payment policy?

_____

What is the cancellation policy?

_____

Are credit cards accepted?

_____

CATERER

Name of catering company:

Name and phone number of contact person:

How many years have you been in business?

What percentage of your business is dedicated to
wedding receptions?

Do you have liability insurance?

Is my date available?

What is the ratio of servers to guests?

What are your extra time fees?

How do your servers dress for wedding receptions?

What menus are available?

Can menus be mixed and matched and/or adapted to fit
within our budget?

Do you offer a menu tasting service, and is there a charge?

_____

What is the price range for:

_____

Seated lunch or dinner?

_____

Buffet lunch or dinner?

_____

Can you provide special meals (vegetarian, kosher, etc.)? If so, at what cost?

_____

Are you licensed to serve alcohol?

_____

What alcohol restrictions are there, if any?

_____

Can we bring our own wine?

_____

What is the corkage fee?

_____

What is your bartending fee?

_____

Are tables, chairs, table linens, glassware, and flatware included in your fee?

_____

Are the table decorations included in your fee?

_____

Are you providing table numbers and place cards?

_____

When is the final guest count needed?

_____

What exactly is included?

_____

Are there any additional fees?

_____

How much is the deposit?

_____

What is the payment policy?

_____

What is the cancellation policy?

_____

Are credit cards accepted?

_____

What percentage of gratuity is expected?

_____

Check and Verify
Table linens and crockery
Tables and chairs

Ask for
Menus and prices

Schedule
Menu tasting

CEREMONY SITE

Name of ceremony site:

_____

Name and phone number of contact person:

_____

What is the minimum and maximum number of guests?

_____

Is there parking space in the vicinity?

_____

Is there handicap accessibility?

_____

Is my date available?

_____

When is the deadline for submission of needed
documents?

_____

When is my rehearsal to be scheduled?

_____

Do vows need to be approved?

_____

What is the ceremony site fee and payment policy? What
is the cost breakdown?

_____

What is the cancellation policy?

_____

Is there any liability insurance?

Is there a civic official available? If so, at what cost?

Are outside civic officials allowed?

Are there any restrictions on music choices?

Are any musical instruments available for our use? If so, at what cost?

Are there any restrictions for photographers/ videographers?

What floral decorations are available/allowed?

Can we bring our own florist to decorate the site?

Can we use rose petals, rice, fireworks, or confetti at the end of the ceremony?

Are candlelight ceremonies allowed?

Are any rental items necessary?

Decorator

Name of decorator:

_____

Name and phone number of contact person:

_____

How many years have you been in business?

_____

What percentage of your business is dedicated to
weddings?

_____

Do you have liability insurance?

_____

Can I see examples of your work?

_____

How much time do you need to set up?

_____

Will you be there on the day?

_____

What are your set-up fees?

_____

What exactly is included?

_____

Are there any additional fees?

_____

How much is the deposit?

_____

What is the payment policy?

_____

What is the cancellation policy?

_____

Are credit cards accepted?

_____

FLORIST

Name of florist:

Name and phone number of contact person:

How many years have you been in business?

What percentage of your business is dedicated to weddings?

Do you have liability insurance?

Can I see examples of your work?

Do you have access to out-of-season flowers?

Will you visit my wedding site and make
recommendations?

Can you preserve my bridal bouquet?

Will you set up the flowers at the ceremony and
reception sites?

Do you rent vases and candelabras?

Can you provide silk flowers?

What other flower arrangements can you provide
(centerpieces, large vases, ceremony decorations, etc.)?

Do you rent plants/flowers in a pot? If so, at what cost?

Will you make a sample bouquet and centerpiece?

How much notice do you need in order to confirm our
order?

How long do you need to set up?

Is delivery included in the final cost?

What are your set-up fees?

What exactly is included?

Are there any additional fees?

How much is the deposit?

What is the payment policy?

_____

What is the cancellation policy?

_____

Are credit cards accepted?

_____

Music/Band/Soloist

Name of musician, band, and/or soloist:

_____

Name and phone number of contact person:

_____

How many years of professional experience do you have?

_____

How many people are in your band?

_____

What type of music do you specialize in?

_____

Can I provide a playlist?

_____

What type of sound system do you have?

_____

Can you act as a master of ceremonies?

_____

How do you dress for wedding receptions?

_____

Can you provide a light and sound show?

_____

Do you have a cordless microphone?

_____

How many breaks do you take? How long are they?

_____

Do you play recorded music during breaks?

What are your hourly fees?

What is the cost of a soloist?

What is the cost of a duo?

What is the cost of a trio?

What is the cost of a quartet?

Do you have liability insurance?

Does the band or soloist need a room to get changed?

How long do you need to set up?

What are your fees and for how many hours?

What is your cost for each additional hour?

What exactly is included?

Are there any additional fees?

How much is the deposit?

_____

What is the payment policy?

_____

What is the cancellation policy?

_____

Are credit cards accepted?

_____

Photographer/Videographer

Name of photographer/videographer:

_____

Name and phone number of contact person:

_____

How many years of experience do you have?

_____

Do you have liability insurance?

_____

Is my date available?

_____

How long have you been photographing weddings?

_____

Can I see some of your work?

_____

Are you the person who will photograph my wedding?

_____

Will you bring an assistant with you to my wedding?

_____

How do you typically dress for weddings?

_____

Do you have a professional studio?

_____

What type of equipment do you use?

_____

Do you bring backup equipment with you to weddings?

Do you visit the ceremony and reception sites prior to the wedding?

Are you skilled in diffuse lighting and soft focus? Retouching?

Do you take studio portraits?

Can I provide a list with desired shots?

What sort of packages do you offer, and what is included?

Do you use proofs, or do you post it online?

How many proofs will I get?

When will I get my proofs?

When will I get my album?

What is the cost of an engagement portrait? Formal bridal portrait?

What is the cost of a parent album?

What is the cost of a five-by-seven reprint?

What is the cost of an eight-by-ten reprint?

What is the cost of an eleven-by-fourteen reprint?

What is the cost per additional hour of shooting at the wedding?

How far in advance do I have to confirm with you?

What exactly is included?

Are there any additional fees?

How much is the deposit?

What is the payment policy?

What is the cancellation policy?

Are credit cards accepted?

Reception Site

Name of reception site:

___

Name and phone number of contact person:

___

How many years have you been in business?

___

What percentage of your business is dedicated to
wedding receptions?

___

Do you have liability insurance?

___

Is my date available?

___

Can the ceremony be held here?

___

Will there be other weddings taking place on the same
day?

___

How much time will be allotted for my reception?

___

Are there noise restrictions?

___

Is there parking space in the vicinity?

___

Is there handicap accessibility?

_____

What is the cost for parking, if any?

_____

Which rooms can we use?

_____

Is there a plan B in case of bad weather?

_____

How many restrooms can we use?

_____

Is the garden/veranda/patio illuminated?

_____

Does the location require a tent or umbrellas? Do I have
to rent them?

_____

Is a dance floor included in the site fee?

_____

Is heating or cooling included in the site fee?

_____

Are tables, chairs, table linens, glassware, and flatware
included in the site fee?

_____

Are the table decorations included in the site fee?

_____

Are you providing table numbers and place cards?

_____

What is the reception site fee?

Are any rental items necessary?

Are there any restrictions for rice, rose petal-tossing, fireworks, etc.?

What is the maximum number of guests for a seated reception?

What is the maximum number of guests for a cocktail reception?

What is the ratio of servers to guests?

What are your extra time fees?

How do your servers dress for wedding receptions?

What menus are available?

Can menus be mixed and matched and/or adapted to fit within our budget?

Do you offer a menu tasting service and is there a charge?

What is the price range for:

Seated lunch or dinner?

Buffet lunch or dinner?

Can you provide some special diets (vegetarian, kosher, gluten-free, etc.)? At what cost?

Are you licensed to serve alcohol?

What alcohol restrictions are there, if any?

Can we bring our own wine?

What is the corkage fee?

What is your bartending fee?

Can you provide customized cocktails?

Are outside caterers allowed?

Are kitchen facilities available for outside caterers?

Are the cake and gift tables included in the package?

What is the cake-cutting fee?

What music restrictions are there, if any?

Are there electric outlets for musical equipments?

Do you have an available sound system? How many microphones are available?

Is there a changing room available?

What is the cost for sleeping rooms, if available?

When is the guests' final count needed?

What exactly is included?

Are there any additional fees?

How much is the deposit?

What is the payment policy?

What is the cancellation policy?

Are credit cards accepted?

What percentage of gratuity is expected?

_____

Check and Verify

Rooms to be used

WCs

Table linens and crockery

Tables and chairs

Ask for

Floor plan

Menus and prices

Schedule

Further visits to the location site

Menu tasting

Rental Supplier

Name of supplier:

_____

Name and phone number of contact person:

_____

How many years have you been in business?

_____

What are your hours of operation?

_____

Do you have liability insurance?

_____

What is the cost per item needed?

_____

What is the cost of pick up and delivery?

_____

What is the cost of setting up the items needed?

_____

When would the items be delivered?

_____

When would the items be picked up after the event?

_____

What exactly is included?

_____

Are there any additional fees?

_____

How much is the deposit?

_____

What is the payment policy?

_____

What is the cancellation policy?

_____

Are credit cards accepted?

_____

Check

All items needed

STATIONERY

Name of stationery provider:

_____

Name and phone number of contact person:

_____

How many years of experience do you have?

_____

What lines of stationery do you carry?

_____

What types of printing process do you offer?

_____

How soon in advance does the order have to be placed?

_____

What is the turnaround time?

_____

What is the cost of the desired invitation?

_____

Announcement?

_____

What is the cost of the desired response card?

_____

Reception card?

_____

What is the cost of the desired thank-you note?

_____

What is the cost of the desired party favors?

_____

What is the cost of the desired wedding program?

_____

What is the cost of addressing the envelopes in
calligraphy?

_____

What exactly is included?

_____

Are there any additional fees?

_____

How much is the deposit?

_____

What is the payment policy?

_____

What is the cancellation policy?

_____

Are credit cards accepted?

_____

TRANSPORTATION

Name of transportation company:

_____

Name and phone number of contact person:

_____

How many years of experience do you have?

_____

Do you have liability insurance?

_____

What types of vehicles do you have available?

_____

Can I see some pictures?

_____

Can you provide a back-up vehicle in case of an
emergency?

_____

How many drivers are available?

_____

How do your drivers dress for weddings?

_____

How much do you charge for waiting?

_____

What is the minimum amount of time required to rent a
vehicle?

_____

What is the cost per hour? Two hours? Three hours?

_____

What exactly is included?

_____

Are there any additional fees?

_____

How much is the deposit?

_____

What is the payment policy?

_____

What is the cancellation policy?

_____

Are credit cards accepted?

_____

WEDDING CAKE

Name of the bakery/wedding cake designer:

_____

Name and phone number of contact person:

_____

How many years have you been in business?

_____

What percentage of your business is dedicated to weddings?

_____

Do you have liability insurance?

_____

Can I see examples of your work?

_____

What are your wedding cake specialties?

_____

Do you offer free tastings of your wedding cakes?

_____

How far in advance should I order my cake?

_____

Can you make a groom's cake?

_____

Do you lend, rent, or sell cake knives, cake pillar, and plate?

_____

When must these items be returned?

What is the cost per serving of my desired cake?

Is there a cake delivery and set-up fee?

What exactly is included?

Are there any additional fees?

How much is the deposit?

What is the payment policy?

What is the cancellation policy?

Are credit cards accepted?

Schedule

Cake tasting

SUPPLIERS
DIRECTORY

ACCOMMODATION

Name_____

Address_____

Website/e-mail_____

Phone number_____

Name of contact person_____

BRIDAL BOUTIQUE

Name_____

Address_____

Website/e-mail_____

Phone number_____

Name of contact person_____

CATERER

Name_____

Address_____

Website/e-mail_____

Phone number_____

Name of contact person_____

CEREMONY SITE

Name_____

Address_____

Website/e-mail_____

Phone number_____

Name of contact person_____

DECORATOR

Name_____

Address_____

Website/e-mail_____

Phone number_____

Name of contact person_____

ENTERTAINER

Name_____

Address_____

Website/e-mail_____

Phone number_____

Name of contact person_____

FLORIST

Name_____

Address_____

Website/e-mail_____

Phone number_____

Name of contact person_____

HAIRDRESSER/BEAUTY SALON

Name_____

Address_____

Website/e-mail_____

Phone number_____

Name of contact person_____

JEWELER/RINGS

Name_____

Address_____

Website/e-mail_____

Phone number_____

Name of contact person_____

MAKEUP ARTIST

Name_____

Address_____

Website/e-mail_____

Phone number_____

Name of contact person_____

MUSICIAN (CEREMONY)

Name_____

Address_____

Website/e-mail_____

Phone number_____

Name of contact person_____

MUSICIAN (PARTY)

Name_____

Address_____

Website/e-mail_____

Phone number_____

Name of contact person_____

OFFICIANT

Name_____

Address_____

Website/e-mail_____

Phone number_____

Name of contact person_____

PHOTOGRAPHER/VIDEOGRAPHER

Name_____

Address_____

Website/e-mail_____

Phone number_____

Name of contact person_____

RECEPTION SITE

Name_____

Address_____

Website/e-mail_____

Phone number_____

Name of contact person_____

REGISTRY SHOP 1

Name_____

Address_____

Website/e-mail_____

Phone number_____

Name of contact person_____

REGISTRY SHOP 2

Name_____

Address_____

Website/e-mail_____

Phone number_____

Name of contact person_____

REGISTRY SHOP 3

Name_____

Address_____

Website/e-mail_____

Phone number_____

Name of contact person_____

RENTAL SUPPLIER

Name_____

Address_____

Website/e-mail_____

Phone number_____

Name of contact person_____

STATIONERY

Name_____

Address_____

Website/e-mail_____

Phone number_____

Name of contact person_____

SECURITY

Name_____

Address_____

Website/e-mail_____

Phone number_____

Name of contact person_____

TRANSPORTATION

Name_____

Address_____

Website/e-mail_____

Phone number_____

Name of contact person_____

TRAVEL AGENCY

Name_____

Address_____

Website/e-mail_____

Phone number_____

Name of contact person_____

WEDDING CAKE DESIGNER

Name_____

Address_____

Website/e-mail_____

Phone number_____

Name of contact person_____

WEDDING FAVORS SHOP

Name_____

Address_____

Website/e-mail_____

Phone number_____

Name of contact person_____

MISCELLANEOUS

BABYSITTER

Name_____

Address_____

Website/e-mail_____

Phone number_____

Name of contact person_____

MASTER OF CEREMONIES

Name_____

Address_____

Website/e-mail_____

Phone number_____

Name of contact person_____

GIFT
REGISTRY

GIFT REGISTRY

In case you forget something, follow the list.

ELECTRONICS AND APPLIANCES

- ☐ Blender/smoothie maker
- ☐ Coffeemaker
- ☐ Countertop oven
- ☐ Dishwasher
- ☐ Dryer
- ☐ DVD player
- ☐ Electric knife
- ☐ Electric skillet
- ☐ Flat screen television set
- ☐ Food processor
- ☐ Hair dryer
- ☐ Hand blender
- ☐ Handheld vacuum cleaner
- ☐ Iron
- ☐ Juicer or juice extractor
- ☐ MP3 players
- ☐ Oven
- ☐ Rice cooker
- ☐ Shower radio
- ☐ Speakers/docking station for MP3 player
- ☐ Stand mixer
- ☐ Stereo sound system
- ☐ Stove
- ☐ Toaster
- ☐ TV set
- ☐ Vacuum cleaner
- ☐ Washer

BATH LINENS AND BATHROOM ACCESSORIES

- ☐ Bath mats
- ☐ Bath sheets
- ☐ Bath towels
- ☐ Bathroom scale
- ☐ Guest towels
- ☐ Hand towels
- ☐ Robes
- ☐ Shower curtain
- ☐ Washcloths

BEDDING

- ☐ Blankets
- ☐ Comforter
- ☐ Duvet cover
- ☐ Fitted sheets
- ☐ Flat sheets
- ☐ Mattress pad
- ☐ Pillow shams

- [ ] Pillowcases
- [ ] Pillows

DECORATION
- [ ] Artwork
- [ ] Carpets
- [ ] Cushions
- [ ] Flower vases
- [ ] Lamps
- [ ] Picture frames
- [ ] Recliners
- [ ] Storage chest
- [ ] Throw for sofa

KITCHEN
- [ ] Assorted spatulas
- [ ] Cake pans
- [ ] Cheese grater
- [ ] Cheese slicer
- [ ] Colander
- [ ] Cookbooks
- [ ] Cookie sheet
- [ ] Crock Pot
- [ ] Cutting boards
- [ ] Dutch oven
- [ ] Fondue set
- [ ] Garlic press

- [ ] Griddle
- [ ] Half sheet pan (aka baking sheet)
- [ ] Ice cream scoop
- [ ] Indoor grill
- [ ] Kettle
- [ ] Kitchen scale
- [ ] Knife block
- [ ] Ladle
- [ ] Loaf pan
- [ ] Mandolin
- [ ] Measuring cups
- [ ] Measuring spoons
- [ ] Mortar and pestle
- [ ] Muffin tin
- [ ] Pie dish
- [ ] Pots and pans
- [ ] Pressure cooker
- [ ] Roasting pan
- [ ] Roasting rack
- [ ] Rolling pin
- [ ] Salt and pepper shakers
- [ ] Set of mixing bowls
- [ ] Skillets
- [ ] Slotted spoons
- [ ] Steamer basket

- [ ] Tongs
- [ ] Whisks
- [ ] Wok
- [ ] Wooden spoons

TABLEWARE
- [ ] Bread plates
- [ ] Buffet site plates
- [ ] Cake server
- [ ] Cereal bowls
- [ ] Cheese knives
- [ ] Corkscrew
- [ ] Covered serving dishes
- [ ] Cups and saucers
- [ ] Dinner plates
- [ ] Five-piece flatware set
- [ ] Ice bucket and tongs
- [ ] Juice glasses
- [ ] Ladle
- [ ] Mugs
- [ ] Napkins
- [ ] Pasta bowls
- [ ] Pitcher
- [ ] Place settings
- [ ] Platters
- [ ] Salad plates
- [ ] Serving set

- [ ] Stemless wineglasses
- [ ] Sugar and creamer
- [ ] Tablecloths
- [ ] Teapot
- [ ] Water glasses/tumblers

TRAVEL
- [ ] Cooler
- [ ] Digital camera
- [ ] Garment bag
- [ ] Suitcases
- [ ] Toiletry kit
- [ ] Travel totes

MY BUDGET WORKSHEET

My Budget Worksheet

Keeping track of all expenses is a major task!

Expenses	Estimated cost	Actual cost
ACCOMMODATIONS		
Hotel (bride and groom)		
Hotel (guests)		
Welcome baskets		
Subtotal		
BRIDAL BOUTIQUE BRIDE		
Wedding dress		
Headpiece/veil/gloves		
Hosiery, undergarments, etc.		
Jewelry		
Shoes		
Dry cleaning		
Subtotal		

BRIDAL BOUTIQUE **MAID OF HONOR**		
Dress		
Subtotal		
BRIDAL BOUTIQUE **BRIDESMAID #1**		
Dress		
Subtotal		
BRIDAL BOUTIQUE **BRIDESMAID #2**		
Dress		
Subtotal		
BRIDAL BOUTIQUE **BRIDESMAID #3**		
Dress		
Subtotal		
BRIDAL BOUTIQUE **GROOM**		
Morning coat/suit/ tuxedo		
Tie/bowtie, cuff links		
Shoes		

Underwear, socks, etc.		
Subtotal		
CATERING		
Food—cocktail, main meal, late meal		
Liquor, beverages		
Bar set-up fee		
Corkage fee		
Rentals (table linen, dinnerware, etc.)		
Table, chairs		
Waiters		
Extra hours		
Gratuity		
Subtotal		
CEREMONY		
Officiant fee and gratuity		
Booklet		

Marriage license and other documents		
Location fee		
Flower basket, ring pillows		
Flowers, aisle runners, candles		
Subtotal		
DECORATION		
Decorator fee		
Decoration items		
Subtotal		
FLOWERS		
Bride's bouquet		
Bridesmaids' bouquets		
Boutonnières		
Flower girls' flowers		
Corsages		
Ceremony site arrangements		

Reception site arrangements		
Centerpieces		
Delivery and set-up fee		
Rentals		
Subtotal		
GIFTS		
Parents		
Bride and groom (each other)		
Flower girls and ring bearer		
Favors		
Subtotal		
HONEYMOON		
Accommodation, transportation		
Luggage		
New clothes		
Subtotal		

Music/ Entertainment		
Ceremony musicians		
Cocktail musicians		
Reception band/DJ		
Entertainers' fee		
Master of ceremonies		
Subtotal		
Photographer Videographer		
Bride and groom's album		
Proofs/digital preview		
Package		
Retouching		
Extra hours fee		
Video		
Disposable cameras		
Subtotal		

RECEPTION		
Reception site		
Food—cocktail, main meal, late meal		
Liquor, beverages		
Bar set-up fee		
Corkage fee		
Rentals (table linen, dinnerware, etc.)		
Table, chairs		
Tent, umbrellas		
Heating/cooling		
Portable WCs		
Parking fee/valet services		
Dance floor		
Wedding cake		
Cake-cutting fee		
Delivery and set-up fees		

Waiters		
Extra hours		
Gratuity		
Subtotal		
STATIONERY		
Save-the-date cards		
Invitations, envelopes, response cards		
Maps		
Menus		
Thank-you notes		
Seating cards		
Programs		
Calligraphy		
Postage		
Subtotal		

Transportation		
Bride's transportation		
Groom's transportation		
Guests' transportation		
Subtotal		
Miscellaneous		
Newspaper announcement		
Prenuptial agreement		
Blood tests		
Taxes		
Wedding rings		
Subtotal		
TOTAL		

SCHEDULE

Schedule

Set up a twelve-month timeline and start planning your wedding. Fill in your plan month by month to begin with and then narrow your plan to weeks and finally to days and hours. Consider the following steps:

Twelve Months

☐ Announce your engagement and intention to marry
☐ Create a wedding website
☐ Choose bridesmaids and groomsmen
☐ Create a guest list database
☐ Create guest lists A and B
☐ Determine the color scheme
☐ Determine your budget and who pays for what
☐ Determine your type of wedding, theme, and
  formality
☐ Enjoy being engaged
☐ Prioritize your different desires
☐ Send mail announcement
☐ Set the wedding date
☐ Start a wedding gifts list
☐ Start looking for reception and ceremony sites
☐ Submit announcement to print publications

MONTH TWELVE

( ) Monday
( ) Tuesday
( ) Wednesday
( ) Thursday
( ) Friday

( ) Monday
( ) Tuesday
( ) Wednesday
( ) Thursday
( ) Friday

( ) Monday
( ) Tuesday
( ) Wednesday
( ) Thursday
( ) Friday

( ) Monday
( ) Tuesday
( ) Wednesday
( ) Thursday
( ) Friday

MONTH ELEVEN

( ) Monday

( ) Tuesday

( ) Wednesday

( ) Thursday

( ) Friday

( ) Monday

( ) Tuesday

( ) Wednesday

( ) Thursday

( ) Friday

( ) Monday

( ) Tuesday

( ) Wednesday

( ) Thursday

( ) Friday

( ) Monday

( ) Tuesday

( ) Wednesday

( ) Thursday

( ) Friday

TEN MONTHS

☐ Book reception site
☐ Choose menus
☐ Choose table linens, tables, and chairs
☐ Contact officiant (civil and religious) and book date
☐ Decide if you will be inviting children or not
☐ Decide on the party scheme
☐ Examine your beauty regimen
☐ Invite flower girls and ring bearer
☐ Make down payment on reception site and sign a contract
☐ Manage your budget
☐ Obtain guests' addresses
☐ Plan your honeymoon
☐ Reserve rental equipment
☐ Select a wedding planner (optional)
☐ Select caterers and sign a contract
☐ Select florist and plan decoration
☐ Select ideas for bouquet
☐ Select ideas for wedding dresses
☐ Select printers

MONTH TEN

( ) Monday
( ) Tuesday
( ) Wednesday
( ) Thursday
( ) Friday

( ) Monday
( ) Tuesday
( ) Wednesday
( ) Thursday
( ) Friday

( ) Monday
( ) Tuesday
( ) Wednesday
( ) Thursday
( ) Friday

( ) Monday
( ) Tuesday
( ) Wednesday
( ) Thursday
( ) Friday

MONTH NINE

( ) Monday
( ) Tuesday
( ) Wednesday
( ) Thursday
( ) Friday

( ) Monday
( ) Tuesday
( ) Wednesday
( ) Thursday
( ) Friday

( ) Monday
( ) Tuesday
( ) Wednesday
( ) Thursday
( ) Friday

( ) Monday
( ) Tuesday
( ) Wednesday
( ) Thursday
( ) Friday

EIGHT MONTHS

❏ Book DJ/band/choir
❏ Define the wedding dress style
❏ Gather ideas for wedding cake
❏ Order tent (optional)
❏ Select a photographer
❏ Select fashion designer, outlet, or bridal boutique
❏ Send save-the-date announcements
❏ Start combining the music playlists

MONTH EIGHT

( ) Monday
( ) Tuesday
( ) Wednesday
( ) Thursday
( ) Friday

( ) Monday
( ) Tuesday
( ) Wednesday
( ) Thursday
( ) Friday

( ) Monday
( ) Tuesday
( ) Wednesday
( ) Thursday
( ) Friday

( ) Monday
( ) Tuesday
( ) Wednesday
( ) Thursday
( ) Friday

MONTH SEVEN

( ) Monday
( ) Tuesday
( ) Wednesday
( ) Thursday
( ) Friday

( ) Monday
( ) Tuesday
( ) Wednesday
( ) Thursday
( ) Friday

( ) Monday
( ) Tuesday
( ) Wednesday
( ) Thursday
( ) Friday

( ) Monday
( ) Tuesday
( ) Wednesday
( ) Thursday
( ) Friday

SIX MONTHS

- ☐ Choose layout for invitations
- ☐ Choose layout for other printed items (optional)
- ☐ Start planning your honeymoon
- ☐ Select florist (bouquet and centerpieces)
- ☐ Register for wedding gifts
- ☐ Obtain marriage licenses
- ☐ Finalize your guest list

MONTH SIX

( ) Monday

( ) Tuesday

( ) Wednesday

( ) Thursday

( ) Friday

( ) Monday

( ) Tuesday

( ) Wednesday

( ) Thursday

( ) Friday

( ) Monday

( ) Tuesday

( ) Wednesday

( ) Thursday

( ) Friday

( ) Monday

( ) Tuesday

( ) Wednesday

( ) Thursday

( ) Friday

MONTH FIVE

( ) Monday
( ) Tuesday
( ) Wednesday
( ) Thursday
( ) Friday

( ) Monday
( ) Tuesday
( ) Wednesday
( ) Thursday
( ) Friday

( ) Monday
( ) Tuesday
( ) Wednesday
( ) Thursday
( ) Friday

( ) Monday
( ) Tuesday
( ) Wednesday
( ) Thursday
( ) Friday

FOUR MONTHS

☐ Arrange accommodations for out-of-town guests
☐ Arrange transportation for guests and the wedding party
☐ Attend wedding dress fitting
☐ Book a room for the wedding night
☐ Buy stockings and special lingerie
☐ Buy suitcase for honeymoon
☐ Choose favors (optional)
☐ Finalize guest lis
☐ Finalize music playlists
☐ Order stationery
☐ Order wedding cake
☐ Purchase or reserve groom's attire
☐ Purchase wedding rings
☐ Start addressing invitation envelopes

MONTH FOUR

(   ) Monday

(   ) Tuesday

(   ) Wednesday

(   ) Thursday

(   ) Friday

(   ) Monday

(   ) Tuesday

(   ) Wednesday

(   ) Thursday

(   ) Friday

(   ) Monday

(   ) Tuesday

(   ) Wednesday

(   ) Thursday

(   ) Friday

(   ) Monday

(   ) Tuesday

(   ) Wednesday

(   ) Thursday

(   ) Friday

THREE MONTHS

- ☐ Choose menus and wines
- ☐ Get passport or travelling document
- ☐ Hire babysitter (when applicable)
- ☐ Keep a record of received wedding gifts and RSVPs
- ☐ Mail and/or deliver invitations
- ☐ Shop for groom's attire
- ☐ Start dancing lessons (optional)
- ☐ Taste wedding cakes
- ☐ Write in database who gave what

MONTH THREE

(   ) Monday
(   ) Tuesday
(   ) Wednesday
(   ) Thursday
(   ) Friday

(   ) Monday
(   ) Tuesday
(   ) Wednesday
(   ) Thursday
(   ) Friday

(   ) Monday
(   ) Tuesday
(   ) Wednesday
(   ) Thursday
(   ) Friday

(   ) Monday
(   ) Tuesday
(   ) Wednesday
(   ) Thursday
(   ) Friday

TWO MONTHS

- ☐ Attend wedding dress fitting session
- ☐ Attend wedding prep sessions
- ☐ Book wedding rehearsal
- ☐ Choose readings for ceremony and select readers
- ☐ Maintain a record of received wedding gifts and RSVPs
- ☐ Make gynecologist appointment
- ☐ Make tropical disease medical appointment (optional)
- ☐ Organize bridal shower for next month
- ☐ Purchase flower basket
- ☐ Purchase or make table signs
- ☐ Start composing table plan
- ☐ Try out first makeup and hairstyle
- ☐ Write wedding vows

MONTH TWO

( ) Monday
( ) Tuesday
( ) Wednesday
( ) Thursday
( ) Friday

( ) Monday
( ) Tuesday
( ) Wednesday
( ) Thursday
( ) Friday

( ) Monday
( ) Tuesday
( ) Wednesday
( ) Thursday
( ) Friday

( ) Monday
( ) Tuesday
( ) Wednesday
( ) Thursday
( ) Friday

WEEK FOUR

☐ Attend bridal shower

☐ Buy and wear wedding shoes twice a week

☐ Buy clothes for honeymoon trip

☐ Buy guest book

☐ Confirm DJ/band/choir

☐ Confirm florist

☐ Confirm honeymoon arrangements

☐ Confirm photographer

☐ Confirm rental equipment delivery date and hour

☐ Confirm wedding cake

☐ Contact guests who didn't respond to invitation

☐ Do beauty treatment

☐ Do blood tests (if required)

☐ Do relaxing massage

☐ Do seating plan

☐ Do second makeup and hairstyle trial session

☐ Go to wedding dress fitting session

☐ Participate in photo testing session

☐ Prepare documents for name change

☐ Print menus and ceremony booklets

WEEK FOUR

(   ) Monday

(   ) Tuesday

(   ) Wednesday

(   ) Thursday

(   ) Friday

(   ) Saturday/Sunday

THREE WEEKS

☐ Attend menu tasting session
☐ Do third makeup and hairstyle trial session
☐ Prepare favors
☐ Send change of address to post office

WEEK THREE

(   ) Monday

(   ) Tuesday

(   ) Wednesday

(   ) Thursday

(   ) Friday

(   ) Saturday/Sunday

TWO WEEKS

- ☐ Attend bachelorette party
- ☐ Attend ceremony rehearsal
- ☐ Confirm and finalize details with officiant (civil and religious)
- ☐ Confirm transportation
- ☐ Have final dress fitting
- ☐ Finalize details with photographer
- ☐ Finalize flower arrangements
- ☐ Pick up groom's attire
- ☐ Review seating plan
- ☐ Select something old, something new, something borrowed, and something blue
- ☐ Wear wedding shoes once a day

WEEK TWO

( ) Monday

( ) Tuesday

( ) Wednesday

( ) Thursday

( ) Friday

( ) Saturday/Sunday

FIVE DAYS

☐ Do reconnaissance trip to ceremony site

☐ Finalize reception seating plan

☐ Finalize seating arrangement

☐ Give musicians a list of your playlists

☐ Inform caterer of exact number of guests

☐ Pack for your honeymoon (clothes, personal and travelling documents, credit cards, and cash)

☐ Pack overnight bags for honeymoon suite

☐ Pick up honeymoon vouchers and tickets

THREE DAYS

☐ Collect wedding gifts from shops
☐ Do beauty treatments session (manicure, pedicure, waxing, relaxing massage, etc.)
☐ Drop wedding accessories and decor at reception site
☐ Make sure you have money in envelopes for tipping
☐ Prepare flower basket and ring tray

TWO DAYS

☐ Prepare survival kit for wedding day
☐ Relax and go for a walk

WEEK ONE

(   ) Monday

(   ) Tuesday

(   ) Wednesday

(   ) Thursday

(   ) Friday

WEDDING DAY

...•... hours Hairdresser appointment

...•... hours Makeup appointment

...•... hours Manicure retouch

...•... hours Snack time

...•... hours Dressing time

...•... hours Photo opp

...•... hours Wedding ceremony

...•... hours Arrival at reception site

...•... hours Cocktail hour

...•... hours Photo op

...•... hours Lunch/dinner

...•... hours Speeches

...•... hours Cake cutting

...•... hours First dance

...•... hours Relaxing at party

...•... hours Departure for honeymoon

After the Wedding

☐ Enjoy every moment of your honeymoon
☐ Renew personal documents
☐ Send thank-you cards for wedding gifts
☐ Pay remaining bills

Be happy